Emergence

Emergence

Jennifer Wenn

First Edition

Wet Ink Books
www.WetInkBooks.com
WetInkBooks@gmail.com

Emergence
by Jennifer Wenn

Cover Design – Richard M. Grove
Cover Image – Richard M. Grove
Layout and Design – Richard M. Grove

Typeset in Garamond
Printed and bound in Canada
Distributed in USA by Ingram,
    – to set up an account – 1-800-937-0152

Library and Archives Canada Cataloguing in Publication

Title: Emergence / Jennifer Wenn.
Names: Wenn, Jennifer, 1959- author.
Description: First edition.
Identifiers: Canadiana 20250126478 | ISBN 9781998324163 (softcover)
Subjects: LCGFT: Poetry.
Classification: LCC PS8645.E53 E44 2025 | DDC C811/.6—dc23

Contents

Portraits II

Empress

Alleyways

Reveries

Contemplations

slender fire races under my skin

Listen to Mother Earth

Listen to Mother Earth

Listen to Mother Earth.
Listen to her breathe.
Listen to a gentle draught
    sigh across a flowering meadow;
to a squirrel tiptoe through foliage;
to an acorn nestle onto embracing soil,
to a welcome shower setting gardens adance,
the pulse of waves rolling ashore,
a burbling creek in attentive woods,
new snow whispering underfoot.

Listen to Mother Earth.
Listen to her call.
Listen to her cry.
Listen to a sere wind rattle through withered underbrush,
then to insatiable fire howl triumphantly
    over acre after doomed acre;
listen to a starving bear tear into suburban detritus,
to the crack and crash of ancient forest guardians
    felled by screaming chainsaws;
listen to rain patter on parched ground,
then to a hail-infused deluge pound the window;
listen to furious gale-driven breakers
    hammer a defenceless coast,
to a roaring flood sweep away all before it,
to sleet and ice rip into naked trees.

Listen to Mother Earth.
Listen.

Strata

Under a louring cloudbank
purblind cars drone by
on the elevated road;
down there a once-thriving pond
is trapped in mortal combat
with invading phragmites.

Fire and Flood

From Australia aflame to
Pakistan drowning, an apocalypse
is shaking itself awake;
whistling past a threatening graveyard
I summon a bubble of
distraction and inattention
but signs and portents
slither in through unseen fissures and
coalesce into dystopian visions:
With Mad Max and Furiosa
I tear around a post-doomsday wasteland
in desperate quest of almighty fuel,
the only real goal to
avoid being vulture food,
but any Pyrrhic desert triumph
is swept away by a nightmarish tempest,
whereupon I join Lear and his Fool
on the blasted heath,
and while the erstwhile king howls
at the gale and deluge I cower,
uselessly,
looking for a sign,
hoping for a sheltering tree
with roots deep enough to
anchor in blazing barrens,
strong enough to
defy the moor-lashing storm,
just one craggy testament of life
while I await the
Godot of tranquillity.

Rose

Red rose gazing up
athirst for precious drops, gift
from far off ocean

Strangler Vine

Suddenly one spring, it was there;
or rather, suddenly noticed:
A snaking strangler vine wrapped
in tight embrace round
an adolescent deciduous tree
seeking only its own space
between the sky-scraping pine and
the cedar hedge's fortress wall,
life clearly sucked from
tree to vine, the former
almost empty, choked off
before it had a chance.

Saving my deciduous meant death for invader;
but maybe the strangler was simply
seizing title to light and life
through brutal efficiency,
conquering in an arboreal competition;
and was it too late anyway?

I ripped out the vine.

An act entwining
hope and vengeance and rescue,
alas not in time, I was told,
best give up and get the chainsaw.

I waited.

Next spring, buds cautiously poked out,
full leaf slowly but duly following,
with no murderous tendril to be seen.
Not yet anyway.

I will be ready.

Crickets

Waiting.
Waiting and listening.
Waiting and listening
      for an unforthcoming answer,
      for an overdue ovation,
      for an absent voice,
with only "crickets" to be heard.
Meaning nothing.
Hence an implied equation: cricket = zero.
But why?
When did song get taken for granted,
exuberant existence fade into a cipher?
For you are there, untiring continuo
on otherwise hushed summer evenings,
needing quiet to be heard.

Cold science points to
      calls for a mate,
      warnings to competitors,
      signals of danger,
      post-concupiscent triumph.
But peace, attend once again,
and find eagerness to chirp along
      when all else demurs,
wings stridulating the night away in
      faithful application to mission,
joy and need in expression.

So sing,
and may we truly hear.

Milkweed

Butterflies dubbed monarch,
wisps of sunrise laced with starry night,
winddancing an impossible migration;
but beauty needs a substrate: enter humble milkweed,
bleeding creamy latex when wounded,
once thriving here and there and elsewhere,
once prized for salve, life-preserver stuffing and more,
then deemed nuisance, tagged for summary extirpation;
those dependent fragile flashes of splendour fading in tandem.

Finally, straws firmly grasped, one incipient fall
six hopeful milkweeds joined my little meadow,
chicken wire protection from the dog,
botanical competition thinned.
Spring saw a return of the special lightish green,
long firm veined ovals reaching out;
alas, no flowers and no seedcases, not yet.
I hovered and tended, waited and pondered.

With a flourishing spread, subterranean rhizomes
announced unseen burrowing come second summer;
and third; and then—fragrant rosy clusters,
thrusting tumescent pods; and a few monarchs.
Late summer's yellowing became autumn brown;
several hulls opened a crack, releasing fluffy messengers
to ride the frosty breeze, but most remained clamped shut.
Winter settled in, chill blasts split some others,
many lost seedlings to fall into a frozen embrace,
lucky ones cradled by the nearby hemlock to await a better fate.
But the determined husks hung on through cold's despond
till the ordained day, only then releasing tufts
of faith and vernal renewal to waft on Nature's breath,
needful spots sought to build anew and
summon again sovereign wonders.

Ode to an "Empty" Lot

Mike my bicycle guy
First made me look.

Seeking a non-literary path to
Reducing head noise,
Prodded by my neglected figure,
I rediscovered two-wheeled pedaling,
Found my way to Mike,
Listened, and followed his gaze:
A green gap in urban concrete
Threatened by all-conquering pavement,
Tagged as empty, but sheltering a
Precious little ecosystem
From grasses to beetles to birds,
A tiny cousin to ancient
West Coast forest sanctuaries
Proffering spiritual serenity
In the face of rapacious chainsaws.
I saw too in Mike's patch a
Mirror of my search's goal,
A precious little interlude of
Peace amidst tumult,
Fragile and fleeting but
Yearning for hope and renewal
In recollection of Limoncocha's
Once decimated primeval jungle,
Now the domain of
Life searching within, recalling the wonder,
Life reaching out in collective resurrection
Of the memory.

The little lot was still thriving,
Last time I went by,
Sending forth optimistic seeds of rebirth,
Corporeal for its modest tract and
Perhaps further afield,
And transcendent ones taking root
In those led to pause and see.

Seasonal Suite

Spring
Welcome at long last,
Ushering winter into rest
After its long labours,
Herald of warmth and verdure
To follow in your wake;
Tarry a while and
Bless us with your
Freshness and hope.

Summer
Freshness and hope
Surges to glorious bloom,
Trees burst to osmose
Sun in full glory, life's
voluptuous high noon;
Vernal descendant,
Infuse us with your
Flowing power.

Winter
Maturity and release,
Guide the sun
Through its nadir,
Wrap us in blankets
Of cold beauty incubating
Hidden, waiting life;
Rest and transfiguration,
Welcome at long last.

Autumn
Flowing power,
Bring forth flaming colour
And groaning harvest;
Gift us with your
Zenithal abundance,
Ease from warmth to
Crisp cool, then soften to
Maturity and release.

Triptychs II

Three Haiku for
the Backyard in August

1

Distinct buzzes all
Round zipline down from the oaks;
Unseen cicadas

2

Humidity cloak
Enfolds, inescapable;
Thunderstorm coming

3

More plops from above;
Acorns searching for bed then
Reawakening

Three Haiku for Warbler Woods

1

Undulating path
Through vernal awakening
Trillium cordon

2

Still unseen souls watch
Nebulous feeling explode
There! Deer flash away

3

Wingèd concerto
Rides woodpecker percussion
Silencing footfalls

Three Haiku for
a Childhood Neighbourhood

1

School's out, kids elsewhere,
Playground's lonely but for me
Breathing in quiet

2

Phantom orchard once
Smiled on this solitary's
Guileless grasps and swings

3

Sporting a bucket
Our maple slowly donates
Sylvan elixir

Three Haiku for
Juno Beach, France

To the Canadians who fought here

1

Birds circle and call
above breakers rolling in;
D-Day ghosts surround

2

That gun emplacement
restored; this one abandoned
to relentless sand

3

Death and heroism
walked these dunes; humble grasses
plead for fragile life

Three Haiku for
Acadia National Park, Maine

1

Scale precipice by
Ladders, rungs and skinny ledge;
Descend easy way

2

Quiet byways once
Tycoon's car-free carriage lanes;
Now plebeians ride

3

Grueling seaside
Hillcrest rewards with hidden
Treasure—blueberries!

Three Haiku for
a Quiet Trail

1

Up lakeside sandhill,
This time follow woods trail and
Find a golf course green

2

Onward alone near
Cliff, each step an adventure;
Skirt poison ivy

3

Gently up and down
Tracking unseen view, then seized—
Sparkling waves, boats, birds

Ekphrastic

Nocturne

*With thanks to those who
saw and captured the magic*

Before, when the sun slipped away
coruscating wonder and wisdom reigned above;
Hablik looked up to find earth grasping
for a whirling, scintillant firmament;
Van Gogh beheld intense, shimmering spirals
of power surmounting a sleepy town;
now, city-bound, I am greeted
by a murky veil harkening
to Whistler's night visions, but
bleached of his delicate beauty.

Abscond, throw off time's shackles,
escape blinding excess;
gaze skyward anew, rediscover the
painful, lost art of
patient, faithful waiting.

[…]

Dusk settles over pastorality,
crickets serenade dancing fireflies,
a dog a farm or two over bids
farewell to the sinking crescent moon
and, channeling Sappho, welcome to
the glittering diamond signifying Venus.
Jupiter, lord of the planets, is soon
shepherded in, followed by the
Martian mote cloaked in dusky red.
The first stars, Dickinson's Arcturus
and Auden's Vega, sparkling across
unfathomable expanses lead a trickle, then
a flood filling the sky with pointillist wildfire
slashed through by the Milky Way's
blazing river of embers.

[...]
[...]
Breathe
[...]
[...]

All too quickly modernity searches me out,
recouples the fetters, and ushers me
back under the cataractic dome,
back to my pseudo-cave where I will
hibernate and remember,
and dream of a return.

Vincent's Stevedores

After The Stevedores in Arles,
by Vincent Van Gogh, 1888

Like oxygen to flame I am swept to radiant
    sunset cradled by a
baroquely ornate frame belying the artist's desperate penury,
museum light playing on crests of strokes bold,
fast and feverish to seize and hold vision and meaning;
for, traverse from sun's glowing adieu across
    the gently flowing Rhone
down to foreground shadows swimming out of
    reflecting water,
watch as they resolve and vitalize into a quay-moored
    boat and workers
racing night to unload coal that will fuel the town behind
while the Trinquetaille quarter on the opposite bank
floats out of silhouette to welcome twilight, my world
merging with the stevedores', unwilling to leave,
unable to pull back, bound into this eternal instant
of light and shade, eventide labour by
retreating solarity, sinking orange morphing
to night-heralding hues overhead,
soft gleams and calls across
brokenly mirroring river,
quiet plish of the coal-boat
rocking gently on its tether,
chink and thump of barrows
wheeled down the gangplank,
low voices that ask and answer, while
nightingale serenades embrace us all;
life in defiance of stalking moonrise.

Pollock's Dance

After One: Number 31, 1950 *by Jackson Pollock*

Up ahead, pulsing on the wall,
lonely, larger than life,
an intricate multi-layered web poised to
ensnare in a fractal labyrinth
vibrating to primeval rhythms;
black, silver and ochre edge splotches
rim a zone where at last a voice
was transiently found away from
addiction's deadly cacophony;
black striations cast
from the unconscious
dash down and diagonal
interlaced with white filigree
weaving a harmonic balance,
ochre stick figures behind the veil
flash in primal surge and flow
with hidden portraits,
all knit together by
teal and gray webbing,
the quiet foundation for
a dance of drip, pour and fling:
gaze down, genuflect and circle your
once and future monumental canvas,
swirl in sub rosa silhouettes,
sling the foundation splashes,
decant knots of pain and joy,
sweep sidestep, sweep sidestep, sweep sidestep,
gently drizzle and dribble,
slash and lash,
lovingly trickle and trill,
skip round and round,
circle and wheel,
coil and meander,

flick step, flick step, flick step,
drip, fling and pour forth
this eternal moment,
a priceless interlude reaped
from a drunken whirlwind,
consuming death defied
by passionate life.

Dr. Goat

After the children's book by Georgiana,
illustrated by Charles Clement

Dr. Goat put on his coat
and we were off again,
rhymes and rhythm carrying me along,
sinking into the warm embrace
of my favourite mythic world
where the sick were healed,
each unique patient,
       mouse, frog, fox and worm,
met where they were,
each one, no matter how diverse,
       from young weasels
       to an elderly elk
       to a high-strung bat
granted their dignity,
for each and all their own custom cure,
       the owl's pink pills,
       a mustard plaster for the walrus,
       the little turtle's cast and
       repurposed roller skate.

When, inevitably perhaps, the physician
who seemed alone was laid low,
his friends, from beetle to chicken,
crept in for succour and support;
the good Dr. G. soon back on his bicycle,
the circle of renewal once more complete,
precious validation to one with
infant memories of dallying at death's door,
a priceless little universe that
retains its place here with me
alongside numerous noble tomes.

Broken Statues

Circling hawk rides on thermals,
casts a piercing glance down and
screeches dominance over human
efforts below, calling to
ancient cousins, raptorial Cassandras
who cried of rises and falls
above then-proud temples and palaces
not yet reduced to Ozymandian Wrecks
vainly trumpeting vanished might and power
and mutely wailing laments for once-dazzling
adornments ravished and broken:
> torsos bereft of a head,
> arms and legs with nothing to carry,
> lovers shorn of embracing limbs,
> staring visages empty of support or context.

I wander amongst these
scraps of shattered beauty now
reverently museum-preserved
remains of a noble past,
flashes of a lost world,
once glorious, then rotting,
finally swept aside and buried by
younger waves, violent, vengeful
neglectful, iconoclastic,
other nations seizing supremacy or
the downtrodden and oppressed rising up,
blazoning new civilizations and
sloughing off these survivors of
> relentless age,
> regime change and insurrection,
> looting and smuggling,
> greed in search of more numerous bits,

all rediscovered and revalued,
what's past and its creators
honoured in atonement for
humankind's variegated destructive impulses;

these fragmentary bequests now
become stepping stones for those
seeking paths to travel back,
drawn by defeated splendour fighting on,
forcing itself into our consciousness,
splinters of a dream we
long to reconstruct and reclaim,
one eroded from physical sight
but flitting in the shadows
      and on vision's periphery,
lurking beneath,
calling from above on waiting wings.

Portraits II

This Moment

For Aunt June

Burdens left behind,
this precious minute
glides into another,
and another,
each released from
the past's restraint,
each free to be what it will,
like a butterfly wafting
through a summer garden,
trusting to divine drafts
for what's to come,
perfect simplicity in
each eternal moment.

Joylyn

You wrote poetry,
were fifty when you came out
> *I am not the man you knew*
> *But a woman, you will meet*
nearly the fifty-three I marked
at my earlier crossing of
that same momentous portal.
Almost two years on we had
never met, only just virtually connected,
so I don't want to presume,
but still, there's a kinship,
both of us trying to write from the heart,
both fated to walk that often-solitary journey,
so yes, there's an ethereal sisterhood
that is with me yet.

You were kind, your friends agree,
a mail carrier who always packed treats
for squirrels along your route.
In pictures I see a gentle soul,
but you fought addiction,
battled bipolar as well,
> *the dark whispers are constant*

So many testify they miss you, but
your *demons* wrapped you in an anguished cloak
> *So lonely is this life*
> *It cuts my soul like a knife*
You fought for the good times,
only to have deadly Hamlet-stained
mists roll in again
> *Oh, to sleep*
> *To dream of loved ones*
> *Where loneliness is vanquished*
> *Where misery holds no sway*

Days after that last poem,
second anniversary of your coming out,
you left us.

I didn't get to know you but
our sisterhood runs deep and so
I peer inside and still, four years later,
find a bicameral waltz
whirling through a noisy throng,
here sad, there angry,
questions with no answers,
fulminations met only by echoes.

Returning to those photos
you look perhaps too gentle for
this journey we did not seek and
which demands so very much,
but then I gaze into the mirror
and wonder if but for a blessing here
or a grace there…

That fateful anniversary you
took the dark path;
made your quietus and
sought the undiscovered country,
the moody Dane might say,
while to me it also seemed you
fell into a Dantean abyss
many can't imagine,
lost the way back,
and left behind hope,
a life unlived,
verses unwritten,
and broken hearts.

May you finally be at peace, Joylyn.

Kaleidoscope for the Invasion of Ukraine, February 24 2022

A murderous despot festers at one end of a ridiculously long table,
    his sycophants huddled at the other.
Tanks grind and clank through the mist.
"Russian warship go fuck yourself."
An obliterated fuel depot shatters the night.
Utter chaos at train platforms leading away from the shells,
    bombs and missiles.
One man blocks a moving tank, pushes on it with his hands,
    and kneels in front of it.
Families and pets jam into a subway station-become-bomb shelter.
An unexploded missile nose down through the pavement.
"The fight is here. I need ammunition, not a ride."
A school with a gaping hole blown through the wall.
Still-smoking wrecked Russian vehicles, bodies splayed alongside on
    the road and a teddy bear mascot from a distant home cowers
    in the dirt and debris.
Young adults march in protest in Moscow despite assurance of arrest
    or beating or both.
A flattened apartment block reduced to dust and rubble.
A mother comforts her disabled daughter in a basement.
Orphaned toddlers hole up with their caregivers in another basement.
A Ukrainian man protests in front of Russian soldiers, a crack,
    he crumples.
A grandmother armed with Googled instructions prepares Molotov
    cocktails in her back yard.
A man climbs onto a moving Russian tank to defiantly wave a
    Ukrainian flag.
A very elderly survivor of the siege of Leningrad protests in St. Petersburg
    with her homemade signs and is bundled off to jail.
Ukrainian mothers pray for their combat-bound sons and knit
    camouflage netting.
At a border railway station a phalanx of baby strollers bestowed by
    Polish mothers awaits fleeing refugees.

A mother and her two children run to cross a road, a missile streaks in and explodes, all three fall dead.

A murderous despot festers at one end of a ridiculously long table, his sycophants huddled at the other.

One Malignant Spirit

Like waves on the ocean
they crest and roll past,
always another in their wake,
tragic echoes of a timeless truth:
just one malignant spirit in power is needed,
       lusting to warp the world
       around hallucination,
       each name a poisonous desecration
       that will not be written here,
just one clawing at all and sundry
       to draw in and corrupt,
       to reveal and empower depravity,
just one to accrete a mob,
       together spawning a
       river of murdered voices
       as singular as bread-line prey of a sniper,
       as multiform as victims in a mass grave.

Consider now that one current driving the deadly flow,
venture upstream in search of the sulfurous source,
follow the meanders and oxbows,
       some fractured and twisted,
       some diseased and septic,
and reach a fault in the substructure
begetting a wellspring for putrescence
to coalesce and ooze into the waters
always questing for release,
       questing for more,
always yearning to dominate and defile;
and when the infernal way is found
lesser spirits are inevitably swept up:
       sycophants, opportunists and true believers;
       blind followers and hordes infected by shadow;
       the fearful and the overborne;
       and legions whose deity is an oath to obey;

all swelling and enabling and reinforcing
the cancerous lodestone devoid of humanity,
        a stranger to compassion, empathy and faith
who sees not people but concepts,
for whom all of us divine sparks
        are merely tools, targets and obstacles,
who would rejoice over Dante's *sorrowful abyss*
        that holds the thunder of infinite screams
        but who the great poet would
        consign to torment eternal,
who yearn to play God but
        who channel only hatred and butchery;
one malignant spirit divorced from light,
just one to find the willing and the weak and more
and bind them in Stygian darkness
that floods out bringing death and despair,
yet one more in a ghastly parade, each
fighting Martin's *arc of the moral universe*,
fighting its endless-seeming curve *toward justice*
that we must struggle for with all we are,
striving for a day when
no malignant spirit can ever again
convulse humankind around their nightmare.

The Ballad of Margaret Murphy

The spring of another century,
an ancient land cherished and
cared for by First Nations
now flooded by waves of settlers
from an ocean away and beyond,
British, Irish and more,
all escaping and searching.

Upper Canada in the newcomers' parlance,
cradled by the Great Lakes, the budding
towns, villages and homesteads
of the 1830's ruled by a masculine
colonialist elite in distant York;
and caught up in the tides of history
was an Irish girl named Margaret.

Rugged Ireland, the Emerald Isle,
home to music, poets and pride,
and, even before the great famine,
home to some lured by opportunity
said to beckon from Upper Canada,
including young Margaret,
a daughter of the prolific Murphy clan.

Fate took her to the heart of the peninsula,
an area replete with United Empire Loyalists
escaping the revolutionary States;
Quakers, Baptists and Methodists
seeking freedom of worship;
site of Norwichville, boasting a tavern,
and so many called the town Sodom.

David Hagerman, born in hilly
Dutchess County New York,
wife Frances and three daughters, 10, 5 and 1;
established in Sodom now, aged 40,
a carpenter, a big man in town;
this David needed a servant, and
Margaret Murphy needed a position.

As summer 1837 faded into fall, Hagerman's
walls hummed with the master's complaints:
The Family Compact in York control everything,
they're corrupt, filched a pile of land
hereabouts for the Church of England;
floors meanwhile hummed with the relentless
swish of Margaret's broom.

Just back from Bedford's Inn, David trumpeted,
William Lyon Mackenzie in York is the hope,
Dr. Duncombe is our man here,
we've got the Norwich Political Union now,
I'm the Quartermaster, we're not letting this stand!
And on it went; what next, wondered Miss Murphy,
crouched low cleaning out the fireplace.

Fall wore into winter, December stole in,
rebel officers met at Hagerman's,
nervous whispers of *but treason?* swept aside by
glorious cries of taking up arms to help Mackenzie,
Duncombe's brigade coming together,
and on it went; trouble, thought Margaret,
cleaning up detritus from the great conclave.

December 12, Margaret, remember this day!
Cross and Davis wouldn't give up their guns
but we got supplies from Wallace's store.
Duncombe has a sword, pistols and a dagger;
Mackenzie's taken York, we are off to capture Brantford!
That's all well and good muttered Margaret,
but I'm off to the laundry and linens.

It's all fallen apart, we only got to Burford,
Mackenzie failed, the Queen's Militia is marching,
Duncombe is a coward and vanished,
Luke Peasley is hiding in a swamp,
I can't stay, the Loyalists are looking for me,
Frances, take care of the girls;
Margaret—you are in charge here now. Farewell.

Rumours were flying through town,
Loyalists said to be on the rampage,
not just hunting men on the run
but scavenging for abandoned loot.
Brave and Hospitable, so ran the Murphy motto.
The first part leapt to the fore;
the second stepped into the shadows.

Floors, fireplaces and laundry
gave way to fearless command,
the day well and truly seized:
If they're coming I need to be ready;
I think I know where he keeps
a couple of convincing helpers.
I'll be damned if that rabble gets anything here!

Wild Irish shores birthed the Murphy name
centuries ago, Sea Warrior the noble wellspring.
A long way from the coasts was Margaret
but the martial blood ran true;
a long way from the ocean and no trident here,
but a land-bound kindred implement
awaited her tenacious grasp.

Up strode the mob, all bluster and swagger,
Hagerman's gone to ground, easy pickings here.
But in the doorway stood an Irish lass,
hair a-billowing, savage look in her eye,
two pistols stuck in her belt,
angry pitchfork primed and ready:
By God you'll get nothing here!

Sweet words and appeals to reason
availed naught but oaths and imprecations;
smirks soon soured to grim realization,
threats beget counterthreats,
haughty barging in quashed by
tines to the throat or a gun barrel to the gut:
You can all go to Hell, you'll get nothing here!

Defeated by implacable feminine will,
would-be pillagers slunk off
in search of easier plunder,
pistols and pitchfork showing them the way,
assorted curses ringing in their ears,
young Margaret looming triumphant,
spirit ablaze with history and the moment.

The government did change, but not yet,
Hagerman caught and tried for high treason;
acquitted, to the shock of many,
returning home to an intact house,
thirty years of a henceforth peaceful life
and a servant named Margaret,
still cleaning, but never the same again.

Hannah's Lament

For Hannah Horsley, my
great-great-great-grandmother

Norwich was my home, looming large in East Anglia,
a different church every Sunday for you
and a different pub every night,
third city in England they say,
with our Castle and Cathedral;
but the twisted, narrow backstreets are what I knew,
with the river cutting through like a jagged blade.

I was born the year of our Lord 1816,
Dad was a gardener for those with money,
Mum's hands were full with all of us kids,
poor St. Benedict's our neighbourhood,
on the west side, just inside the old city wall,
where everyone just tried to make their way,
where the river wasn't far, always whispering
a gentle siren call, but Mum kept us away.

Oldest girl I was, and so Mum's helper,
cleaning, cooking, looking out for the little ones,
but I learned to read and write, proud of that I am,
was nobody's fool, and so when I caught
Thomas Horsley's eye, a coppersmith like
his father John, well, I knew a good thing, I thought;
we married September 1837, the river just
a sigh a few streets over.

To Heigham we moved, just outside the old wall,
two madhouses near by, as poor as St. B's,
yet near work and Thomas' folks,
and what we could afford; but low-lying,
damp and foggy the air, for the river, slinking
here and there through swamp and marsh,
was close.

Our children started coming, I loved them all,
but little Edward, oh, he was special,
right until he fell ill and we lost him, just three years old;
we are sorry, but God's will they said, *the others need you,*
they urged, *young Harriet and little Tom;*
but I had trouble hearing through the
pain and the crying of the river.

Came 1846 Thomas' Mum gave up the fight,
all swollen and bedridden, and so John now alone;
money getting scarcer, the Hungry Forties
they called them, and they sure bit hard;
Thomas, he kept at it, when the work was there,
but with one thing and another the idea made sense:
Move in with John, not far, nearer yet to the creeping flood.

Another son! Spitting image of our lost one,
so we named him Edward as well.
But the river flowed on: Thomas lost his job,
started over as a bricklayer's labourer
while I kept the children fed and clothed
in the shadow of the beckoning waters.

Like a thief in the night it came,
September, 1854; John took sick,
the Cholera they said. Terrible his suffering,
his insides trying to get out; nothing worked,
he soon turned blue as the ocean, then was gone.
Three days later, and I'll never forget,
I don't feel well Mum, Edward moaned;
and soon he was in bed listening
to the river slip away.

Typhus this time, they said, and soon
he was burning up, then the rash came;
weaker by the hour, didn't know where he was
or anything else. Thomas and I stayed round the clock,
but nothing worked, and soon my second Edward,
like the first, was gone, and heard only
the hymn of the river.

We are so sorry, they said, *but now*
young Harriet and little Tom still need you.
Thomas, he tried too, and I listened, but
in the still of the night I visited the river, and
when the moon was right, a quarter full and growing,
I could see my babies.

We flowed onward a year and more,
to the spring when my first Edward
would have been fourteen, and
the day when the second was eight;
I went down, I could feel them there,
but the moonlight was yet a tad weak.

Eleven more days, June 8, waxing quarter moon,
fine early summer's evening, I slipped away along
the familiar path, and there they were,
my Edwards, in the summoning water, and
when the nightingale rested I could hear them call,
asking for Mum. All else, any thought of future,
of my poor Thomas, or Harriet and Tom,
faded into the gathering gloom and I
fell into the river's embrace,
reaching out for my lost dear ones,
borne down by the past and its struggles
like an anchor.

And when the moon is right, and the air is quiet,
if you can still find the spot and
the river is willing, you just might see
a mother and her sons locked
in an eternal embrace.

Postcard Home, February 14 1917

For Frank Hill, cousin of my maternal
great-grandmother Josepha Mason

Dear Cousin Sephie

> Francis William Hill, known to everyone
> and in many records as Frank

Rec. your welcome letter a few days ago

> Born Windham Township, Ontario
> August 14, 1890

Was pleased to hear from you all

> Marital status: single
> Occupation: farmer

Was very sorry to hear of Becca being so bad

> Height: five feet, four and a quarter
> inches

Well, I am still in England

> Complexion: fair
> Eyes: blue
> Hair: light brown
> Marks: Operation scar hernia, operation
> scar appendix

but I don't think it will be for long

> Service Number: 797515
> Rank: Private

Would like to write you a letter

> Next of kin: Esther Emilia Hill, mother

but can't get the time just now to do it

> April 4 1917, arrived in France and joined
> the 123rd Canadian Pioneer Battalion

It keeps me busy answering letters & cards when I get a little time

> May 18th 1917, transferred to the 29th
> Battalion,
> 6th Canadian Infantry Brigade,
> 2nd Canadian Division

We are working longer days now

> Fought at the Battle of Hill 70, which between August 15th and 25th, 1917, pitted the Canadian Corps against divisions of the 6th German Army near Lens, France

I am well hope you are all the same

> With his division and the 4th Canadian, assaulted and captured Hill 70 itself, and repelled 21 German counterattacks

Tell Eliza I will write to her again

> The fighting was brutal, even by the standards of the time

Glad to hear that Bob isn't getting thin

> Went on the attack again on August 21 in the assault against the town of Lens

Good Bye from Frank

> August 21, 1917, killed in action, aged 27.

> Frank's body was never found, and consequently you will find his name engraved on the Canadian Vimy Memorial, along with more than 11,000 others from that war, whose mortal remains were similarly lost forever.

> Rest in peace, Frank.

(Un)Damaged Goods

Look in the mirror and you will see
strength, beauty, vigour;
certainly I do, and the world with me.
But it seems there's more, lurking somewhere,
that surfaces in vulnerable moments:
Memories of an emergent young woman, and
memories of another who in his
     weakness and shame and depravity
tried to rob you of innocence and joy,
tried to tag you with a notice marked
     Damaged Goods;
a label that never remotely fit,
     not at any point.
Oh, there was a time you felt it indelible,
but we both know it was never there,
though the thought once burned you
     like a brand.

And now, bask in the wisdom
that is innocence transmuted,
revel in joy, and keep shining
that sacred light that is yours alone.

The Hunter

After Metamorphoses, *by* Antoninus Liberalis, *which contains
the only Greek mythological reference (a brief one) to Siproites*

Just south of ancient, fabled Crete,
fifty stadia and a few more,*
reposes a little rocky uninhabited pair of islets
named Letoa, after immortal Leto, seduced by Zeus
and chased the world over by jealous Hera;
these barren outcrops Leto's refuge to bear divine twins:
Dazzling Apollo, god of music, dance and prophecy,
lord of healing and poetry;
and noble Artemis, fiercely virginal
goddess of the hunt, young women and chastity,
mistress of animals and the wilderness.

Artemis loved to roam Crete's mountains and valleys,
bow in hand, stalk the deep forests and ravines,
luxuriate in clear waters far from mortal habitations
where resided both newly-arrived and enduring families.
One clan, long replete with artists, seers and healers,
venerated her sibling Apollo especially;
all but Siproites, called son and brother,
whose heart stood apart, never at home,
even when cocooned with family doing ritual obeisance,
a solitary amidst the Apollonian throngs.
Ceremonies over, Siproites' feet would
drift away from that shrine
to the now-quiet Temple of Artemis,
irresistibly drawn to her great statue,
and then stare long in confusion and wonder
until, prompted by an unnameable torment,
would seize a great bow and in emulation
strike out, but alone, into the woods,
lithe and graceful,
dancing over roots and rocks,

* *About ten kilometres*

slipping through tangle and thicket,
hunting always and only the great stags
till driven home by a sought-for
but punishing exhaustion.

One summer's day, finding neither prey nor peace,
Siproites wandered far, over a forested crag
and into a hidden gorge, thinking to find
renewal at a summoning stream.
Parting a curtain of tall ferns
Siproites froze in amazement, for there,
bathing in the clear waters,
none other than Artemis herself,
revealed in all her glory.
Their eyes locked for a moment,
awe and a sudden flash of envy momentarily
coursing through human veins until
Siproites in shame averted the gaze and
stammered out an apology for
rudely but accidentally intruding
on her divine tranquillity.

Artemis regarded the quaking mortal
for long seconds, finally speaking slowly:
> *No, indeed you are not like some who*
> *think to violate and hence suffer;*
> *but no man can see me thus and*
> *remain living as he is;*
at which Siproites' head drooped further
in trembling acknowledgement,
> *but I have seen into your heart,*
> *travelled its veiled byways,*
> *found its lost trails, and*
> *the riddle they encompass*
> *answers all, for you are no man.*
With that Artemis waved an imperious arm and
transmuted Siproites' outer form to a glorious feminine,
stunning her with coruscating, transcendent waves of

fire
> shock
>> bewilderment
>>> denial
>>>> release
>>>>> revelation
>>>>> relief
>>>>>> acceptance
>>>>>> and celebration.

Finally regaining speech, Siproites dropped to one knee:
> *I have no words except to ask for some way*
> *to show inexpressible gratitude.*

Artemis in turn extended a hand:
> *Rise and follow. One quest for you has ended;*
> *hunt with me from now on.*

> Postscript:
> *The Cretan, Siproites, had also been turned*
> *into a woman for having seen Artemis*
> *bathing when out hunting.*
>> *The complete reference, from*
>> Metamorphoses,
>> *by* Antoninus Liberalis

Empress

The highly controversial Roman leader known to us as Elagabalus
was born about 203CE in Emesa, Syria, and became ruler of
the Empire in 218CE at age fourteen

Denarius
Call me Empress.
That feels right;
not Emperor as
all designate me.
Some years ago the throne
became mine.
Proof is in my hand:
a little silver denarius,
day's wage for a foot-soldier,
sporting my profile,
youthful, pretty,
laurel wreath of course
(alas for a tiara)
and my eyes,
soft, ample,
looking for answers;
no, searching first for questions:

> **Silk**
> Sublime Emesa,
> far east of the Imperium,
> clothed in smooth Syrian silk,
> not rough Roman wool,
> a century and a half after glorious Trajan
> the cradle for my inception into
> a noble family who called me
> (their son and grandson) Varius.
> Emesa, home of refinement and sensuality,
> receptive to feminine spirit and power,
> I honour you.

Dance

Through a distant mirror
I recall a beautiful child;
journey back, and feel
gentle robes confer
a modicum of peace,
but a voice still called,
a veiled ghost still haunted,
so I danced and let it sweep me away,
lost in the shimmer and whirl
skip and leap into a priceless moment
melding with swish and sway
hidden from nameless longings
that wait to push and pull.

Chosen

Family helms one's fate,
or tries to, some say;
Grandmother (sister-in-law and
aunt to Emperors),
ever ready to grab the tiller
and steer us into a storm;
Father too busy and distant,
dead for good when I was twelve;
Mama, always nearby,
bestowing the hereditary
high priesthood of Elagabal,
Emesa's deity and gift to the world,
the sun supreme,
his great bequest a
simple-looking black conical stone,
but our holy baetyl
offering communion
through splinters of Elagabal's glory
clasped in its bosom and

demanding rites ecstatic and exotic.
To channel this truth,
shine this light,
above all others I am chosen,
destined from birth.

Purple
The sovereign moment comes,
driven by Grandmother's
relentless plotting
in quest of the crowning purple,
putting it about royal cousin Caracalla,
a year murdered and
two Emperors ago,
had an illegitimate son:
namely me;
another role I embrace.
First, charm the legions,
for everyone and everything
tells me I am destined
and ready to be Emperor myself,
to stand, young as I am,
manly and proud astride
the civilized world;
all save the soft spectral voice
I will banish.
We ride then, fly forth
to battle at Antioch,
Gannys, my tutor, our newly anointed
yet suddenly brilliant general;
but at the crisis
Mama and Grandmother
take the field, rally the troops,
and I charge at the head,
sword held high,

cleaving bodies and
flashing at ghostly whispers
until the setting sun
bled out and engulfed
me in purple.

Unfettered

I am now styled
Marcus Aurelius Antoninus,
Antoninus for short
(that's on my coins too),
duplicating cousin Caracalla's
regal label.
Another mask.
But everyone bows down to it;
to me!
Has the world gone mad or
suddenly right-side up?
Unfettered, blinding opportunity blazes forth,
Rome and its overpowering
maleness needs shaking up:
I will keep my "barbaric"
silk and flowing robes;
host parties unlike any other;
bring Elagabal's exotic rites
to a new home;
and why not women in the Senate,
starting with Grandmother and Mama?

Solstice

Mama is right,
a sacred mission calls:
unify all deities under
Elagabal's glorious light,
now also known as Sol Invictus,
Undefeated Sun.

The Elagabalium, right on
Palatine Hill, is ready for
our sacred baetyl.
Summer solstice will be the
wondrous moment, the great festival,
the baetyl borne by a
golden, jewel-encrusted chariot
drawn by six horses, huge
and pure white, guided
by Elagabal's own unseen hand.
I myself will lead the way,
always facing the divine glory,
back to the road ahead;
all senators will watch in awe
as I dance round the altar;
I will declare universal joy
leavened with free food for the people.

Mystery
They haunt me day and night,
flesh-and-blood avatars of
Venusian sanctity
replete with
       boundless soft curves,
       skin smooth as Emesan silk,
       melodious voices,
       and the intoxicating cleft
       of glorious, subtle beauties;
I surround myself with them
but long to possess all of it,
long to be so desired and celebrated,
to be at the centre of such
a wonderful mystery.

Divinity

A thousand curses on sensibilities
and proper decorum!
I <u>will</u> perform on the stage,
just a sideways step from
what I do every day,
but this time I shall be
the Goddess of Love herself,
the immortal feminine
shining through me; but more,
let divinity use my body,
divorce the wife I took to please them,
marry a forbidden Vestal Virgin
(damn the consequences,
Rome needs remoulding),
have deified children,
continue Elagabal's holy mission
of unification.

Search

No one understands.
More wives in succession, yes,
but still I search, hunting for
the image to embrace that
will make me whole,
the spirit to clasp
that will bring me peace,
and cannot find it;
back to my Vestal Virgin.

No one understands.
Grandmother grasps for control,
longs to pull the strings,
but I've severed them:
I rule, not her!

And she of all people should
understand the murders; that's how
the Imperial game is played:
threats, even named Gannys,
removed; throne safe.

Torment

In ages hence, contemplating
my profile, will you see it?
My ghostly childhood voice in full cry,
dances now unavailing,
the torment unceasing,
unnameable, unbearable;
I yearned to understand, to sympathize,
so I befriended harlots,
freed some who were enslaved;
I burned to prove my beauty
    and enflame with desire
so I lived through them;
all not enough, never enough,
I am consumed to ashes with
the hunger to feel as they do,
to know what they were born with:
half the Empire to the physician
who can gift me with my own vagina!

Obeliscus

I found it, restored it, erected it:
Hadrian's vanished monument to
his lost beloved, the virile Antinous;
that obeliscus now stands proudly
at the Circus Varianus,
glistening gloriously seductive
pink after sunshowers,
doubling as a tribute to

my own virile beloved Hierocles
whose passion I constantly ache
to penetrate my inmost being,
for whom I long to prove
wife and queen
(for those are the words that call out),
and more, for the world
to rise up and celebrate us!

Finis

And now, the Empire is stable but
like some reborn Hydra,
the poisonous jaws are
endless, relentless,
and won't stay dead:
my Hierocles not acknowledged;
formal power for women still resisted;
the Roman elite still clinging to their
motley crew of gods and goddesses,
my great union under Elagabal
not countenanced;
my inborn difference not understood
    and a torment worse by the day;
and Grandmother plotting again,
this time to cast me aside,
forcing my other cousin Alexander,
    four years younger and more pliable,
on me as heir (transparently, the
lethal knife hovering nearby).
In time-honoured Roman fashion
I tried an assassination, but Alexander still lives;
the ever-fickle Praetorian Guard now
demand to see Mama and me.

Why, I wonder, did all this come
to the beautiful twirling child I once was?
Only Elagabal knows that.
Oh, we will go to the Praetorians;
I fear they lie in wait,
but go we must,
our path is laid,
I will make the attempt.
If the worst happens, what then of
my memory, what will become of that?
Violated and besmirched, I suspect; but
if not now, then some day,
may my legacy triumph.

Look at my denarius
and know I tried to
turn the world right-side up;
consider the little coin again, and know
Rome once had a young, beautiful
Empress from far-away Emesa.

Elagabalus (a name not given to her until after her death) was murdered at age eighteen along with her mother, on March 11, 222CE, by the Praetorian Guard. Their bodies were dragged through Rome and dumped into the Tiber River.

In November, 2023, the North Hertfordshire Museum in Hitchin, a town north of London, England, reclassified Elagabalus as a transgender woman and indicated that they would henceforth use the pronouns she/her.

Alleyways

Alleyways

Once, I knew them all,
slipped through downtown's capillaries
without a care, escaped into
gaps between edifices,
relished my secret
mastery of shortcuts.
Then, relentless time and a
gender presentation flip
did away with my entitlement
and I wouldn't hazard them anymore.
Some routes are gone now,
but, in the survivors,
once-sheltering walls
see me differently, quiet
now breeds a feared unknown,
private respite from the crowd
now darkened to lonely dread,
where once I hunted
a small adventure
now I would be the prey.

Oh, I still explore, solitary,
but these days my lanes
are incorporeal, they slide
in and around the typical,
searched-for fissures in the
edificial majority,
hidden connections between
my psyche's sequestered bastions,
lost paths to secret memory
still being refound.
All these seams of wisdom
beckon to this remade,
aging adventuress,
more alleyways, ethereal ones,
calling out for discovery.

Me and My Shadow

In acknowledgement of the song lyrics by Billy Rose

Banished but never gone,
melded with deepest midnight but
still stalking, waiting;
till one day, an interval of
attempted peace,
attempted connection to
long-benighted and -berated body,
became chosen moment for a push back
into my consciousness by this
long-repressed revenant,
shadow of interred pain,
a menacing persona attempting
return from outer darkness then
retreating before identity discovered,
mockery resumed once more.
Strolling down avenues of memory,
finding it always there,
shapeless and ancient,
my ever-present companion
always out of reach,
shrinking from any grasp,
impenetrable and spectral,
features formless as twilight mist,
hidden from all light,
stage-whispering from its lair during the day,
slithering out when shades of night fall
to frolic at the dreamworld masque,
triggering all manner of waking
speculation on known remembrance,
none fit for dark purpose.
Elder recollection tosses clues
but revelation remains

abyssal deep, refusing to surface.
Sibilant murmurs suggest delusion but
a clear little voice insists on lost truth
while me and my shadow
haunt each other in mutual incomprehension,
one little figure hovering in a corner.

Appendectomy

After Gwendolyn MacEwen

Gwen's scar was *diagonal and straight…*
parallel to the hip, a perfect geometry;
and something worth bragging about.

Mine, however, is the offspring of a new technique,
reticent, or maybe subtle, a little curve
just underneath the umbilicus,
a tiny snippet from a Pollock fractal web
pulling in loops and whorls of memory:
>My family doctor over the phone,
>*get to emerg, now.*
>[…]
>De rigueur anti-Covid masks everywhere.
>[…]
>The man in the bed next to me in the ER ward
>describing ghastly-sounding leg putrescence.
>[…]
>The lady two beds over nearly deaf and
>evidently without her hearing aids.
>[…]
>*Jennifer, we have to operate immediately, but*
>*need your consent, noting you may*
>*die on the operating table.*
>[…]
>Struggling awake in an over-capacity recovery room, one
>inmate detailing his digestive difficulties to a nurse.
>[…]
>*Jennifer, your appendix was in really bad shape but*
>*we got to it just before it burst.*

Indeed, my scar is written more
on the spirit than the body,
necessitating a different sort of boasting than Gwen's
(but I try).
And my surgeon? All I really know is her transcendent artistry.

Unseen Agonies of a Poet

Comma? Semi-colon? Dash?
Go all out with a period? Too much—
throttle back a bit to a colon?
No, that's a different kind of flow.
But then, so is a dash, arguably
(unless you use it like Emily Dickinson).
So would parentheses help? Doubtful.
Focus. Simplify—
or, simplify: comma or semi-colon?
Wait, could maybe just change the
location of the line break.
Oh hell; let me scroll on my phone
for a bit…hang on, could use an ellipsis.
But that feels wrong somehow…

Triplicity

Regarding a Housefly

Held in the close embrace of early July heat,
birdsong serenades float from the oaks
down to the patio where I meander through
Love Poems from God,
glasses propped on forehead and
book held close in deference to myopia.
Eyes flick up and are greeted
by an alighting Musca domestica,
a housefly doing a high-wire on the page edge.
We tarried there a good ten seconds
(four hours in fly-time),
eyeball to ommatidia, while its back legs
scissored together in fly-thian ritual ablution,
a tiny embodiment of change
semaphoring "take time to notice,"
a strange forerunner preaching awareness.
Task fulfilled she (I feel sure about that)
zipped on her way, leaving me with the
other seraphic poems.

Death in the Afternoon

With apologies and thanks to
Ernest Hemingway and Seamus Heaney

Summer's dénouement was the wasps' cue.
In turn I had (cleverly I thought) baited a fancy trap,
and started this sunny afternoon
contentedly eyeing casualties.
Next to the watering can, startled by a
large arthropodic drowning victim.
Per 2020 my thoughts raced to
It's a murder hornet(!).
Per my more grounded Millennial son,
it was a cicada.
Then past skittering chipmunks grown
smug since Marcus reached the canine beyond,
and to the lower part of my haven
for some quality time with a lawn chair
and Seamus Heaney.

[…]

The imperious *floop* over my left shoulder
startled me out of glorious poetic lyricism
into conjunction with its material embodiment:
not five feet away, base of the stairs
down from the arbour, a magnificent red-tailed hawk
glowing with athleticism and inevitability,
an artist in his realm bristling with
deadly intensity in this moment,
had swooped underneath the oaken canopy
and was now clutching a formerly
complacent chipmunk in his talons.
I was well and truly seen,
pinioned and humbled and

yet comforted under his penetrating gaze,
induced to remain basking in
eloquent physicality until one majestic
motion launched him away.
Feeling the book again in my hands,
swathed in Seamus' ethereal smile.

Tierce

To the backyard, virtual employment left inside,
mid-September glowing all around
while I drifted off to a poetic confrontation
with a ghastly shade haunting a dark literary mountain
whose ascent required grappling with the lost soul
responsible for monstrous evil, finding myself
drifting in Blakean imagery as I searched for a route
to portray an inhuman, warped psyche.

Filtering through the struggle, the gentle rattle
of a small foot on the eavestrough, then a
hopeful fluttering as I glanced up
to find a young cardinal touching down
scant inches away on the patio table.
Startled back to sunshine,
caressed by an inquiring, nascent look,
I said hello, was answered by
a wing-borne dancing spirit
radiating little seraphs of light that
illumine those dark crags winding upwards.

After an infinite moment of communion
the herald was off to the cedar hedge,
leaving me a path, discernible, daunting and destined.

Crossing Lines

I am a trans person,
and thus for some have crossed a line,
become an unwanted, disruptive element
crashing the party of their comfortable psyches.
It was not always thus;
so long as my male avatar soldiered on,
so long as my female truth remained
    bound and gagged,
they were not disturbed.

But this is not a whim or a whimsical choice,
not some neurotic obsession;
rather, beyond psychology or sociology,
deeper than marrow,
this is our very soul, my very soul,
so eventually and inevitably,
while chanting *To thine own self be true*
a flaming sword sundered her bonds
    and out she strode,
only to be deemed a line-violator,
and, for its guardians, morph into a
respect-free other, worthy only
of glares or maybe a
malicious shout of "Tranny!"

Nevertheless, she persisted, has since
claimed a domain, found support,
found friendship and community,
but threats may lurk in any space, any encounter,
like the vigilante at World Pride
who figured I'd crossed a line into
being property, and in broad daylight
smugly grabbed my crotch.
In darkly satisfying fantasies
I drilled him in the gonads or
slapped his smirk into next week;

reality was sitting there being
consoled by a young lady saying
Don't worry, he always does that.

But look around, I am only one person,
look around and find that my vigilante's
contagion is still very much here,
flowing from the mouths and pens
of malignant bigots ranging from
so-called comedians who mock us
to wealthy authors who deny we even exist
to an adult film star ranting for us to be lynched;
all this despite ostensible improvements and
blossoming visibility.

So yes, look around, as I am just one woman,
better off than most of my trans family;
many run gauntlets I am spared
due to privileged location and economics;
to my, and society's, shame, my Caucasian
skin colour confers benefits;
and unlike a few folks I know
I have not been beaten.

Now gaze farther afield over our oft-dangerous globe
and find it is easy to descry locales dominated by
those aghast at our audacity in merely being,
who scoff at *lesser* and prefer *abomination,*
eyeing a hell-hole jail or execution
to obliterate our transgression
of their warped boundaries.

But officialdom is not the end of it;
too many of us, wherever we are,
incur the deadly wrath of the mob
or the lone predator.
Witness Dwayne, not so many years ago:
What line did she cross?

Wanted to socialize as herself, for the first time.
Consequence? Beaten, stabbed, shot and run over
by self-appointed defenders of gender.
Final words as she stood her ground? *I'm a girl!*
And here is Nikki, much more recent.
Her line? Went on a date.
Upon trans identity being disclosed
her sensitive companion felt no option but to
strangle her with a phone charger cord and
dump her on a hillside.
Or consider Alexa, homeless, who was
hunted down and assassinated for
the unpardonable sin of using the ladies' room.
And on and on the blood-soaked list goes.

Dwayne, Nikki, Alexa,
just three of far too many.
I honour them and their bravery,
I cry out that they blessed Creation
    with priceless value and meaning,
I refuse to forget their senseless, tragic and
    often horrific deaths,
I mourn lives cut far too short,
I mourn potential unrealized,
I mourn for those who cared about them,
I weep for their awful suffering,
I rage and howl at a world that still
    harbours hatred such as this.

My name is legion hissed the demon,
and some would cast us in the same role,
would likewise cast us into swine to be drowned,
but we aren't going anywhere,
for we are children of God, we are a host
demanding the erasure of all those infernal lines,
demanding an end to the hatred and violence,
demanding justice for the victims and
    judgement for the guilty,

demanding space free from fear alongside everyone else,
celebrating our wondrous and excruciating journeys
    and the wisdom only they can bring forth,
celebrating our incomparable beauty and strength,
for yes, we are a host, living and spirit,
with gifts for humanity beyond measure
that was in the front line at Stonewall
then somehow pushed off the progress train,
but no more, never again,
we aren't going anywhere,
for yes, we <u>are</u> children of God, we are a host
demanding the eradication of those infernal lines,
demanding an end at last to the hatred and violence,
demanding justice now for the victims and
    judgement for the guilty,
demanding space for all of us free from fear,
celebrating our wondrous and excruciating journeys
    and the wisdom only they have brought forth,
celebrating our incomparable beauty and strength,
for yes, we are a host with gifts for humanity beyond measure
and we will finally claim <u>our</u> place in the sun,
indeed we will haunt the earth till doomsday
in unceasing quest of that better tomorrow.

Reveries

Memento Reverie

A time before time,
spectral and yet existent,
out of mists and aether
shadows crystallize and anneal,
an ancient emergence made new,
and, nascent, I am there.

Transfigure to temporal, build and flourish,
burgeoning material and materiel
enswirl with enlightenment and vision;
grasp light in defiance of darkness,
divine the secrets,
and, novitiate, I am there.

Amidst endless-seeming radiance
comes the warning, stark and final:
midnight is on the prowl.
The great command:
preserve our essence, emblazon the annals,
secure them safe from maelstrom.
The light then transformed
to darkly lustrous runes,
lovingly, fearfully, dauntlessly
implanted in a chamber deep;
and, suddenly venerable, I am there.

An age slips away under
brilliant, blinding night,
much seemingly gained,
much apparently lost,
new veneers piled layer on layer
over truth forgotten but
yearning still for release,
waiting for advent of revelation,
yearning for me to be there.

Ghostly apparitions beckon,
once-mute bones begin to whisper,
an inevitable, long-awaited
excavation bores ever inward
to a hidden catacomb
cradling inscrutable memory
that defies easy epiphany;
and I appear, because I know,
only I now know, for
realization dawns that
I was there.

Moon Song

With thanks to Stephen Sondheim

Casting for the musical is underway,
roles and pieces doled out
like manna from heaven to be
prepared, presented and savoured,
and I cast a disinterested, off-key eye,
only to be corralled and
handed sheets headed
> *Send in the Clowns*
> *(second act climax)*

Thinking Sondheim's shade surely
would be aghast, I protested
my vocal affinity to a dying goat;
and thus cued Art, the high school drama guru,
to sail in on a wave of summoning voices
with a forceful dissent that
left me no choice but to
swim in the lyrical pool;
> *Me here at last on the ground,*
> *You in mid-air*

floats by and I see Art's point,
I am out of sync, out of time,
recurring pattern, so who better?
Singing at the Gala Premiere
I sound uncannily like Judy Collins,
divine feminine sadly assuming mockery,
> *But where are the clowns,*
> *Send in the clowns,*
> *Don't bother, they're here*

the weight of it all
dropping me to the stage
in an emotional full-court curtsy
which prompts wild applause

and an encore;
resonance echoes the tableau
over and over
until my post-closing speech's
musings on age and
how long can I perform,
but *she is so much a part of me* I say,
continuance beckoning from the wings.

Emergence

Searching through the fragments of my dream shattered sleep
Gordon Lightfoot, "Carefree Highway"

1

Out of abyssal silence
and stygian nightmare
two figures trailing
miasmic streamers of dread
emerge and approach,
wordlessly weaving an
indissoluble web, binding
all of us, adults and one child,
to their plea, and
we answer, we agree;
this dyad must be saved.

2

Urgent debate, how to proceed,
we must escape, we must journey;
one voice urges west,
the most direct route home;
we acquiesce, and set out,
walking the misty road, and
sweep up other wanderers
into the mission.
We are now ten, a
decuplet of seeking spirits.

3

Footsore, we glance back, are
greeted by gaining darkness—
we must go faster.
A car is willed into existence,
miraculously we all fit,
although my hat is too distinct,

it must be removed,
we must conceal our purpose,
our numbers call attention,
I will hold the child close,
blend together,
one who speaks the language will drive,
I sit back right
and we hurry away.

4

We are tired,
we are exposed;
there—isolated and deserted,
a small villa,
refuge from chaos and danger.
We slip in for a
moment
of
peace.
[...]
Alarm!
They come! Hide!
I disappear into a bed,
my head to the foot,
cower to shut it out,
slide into saving
transfiguration and transposition.

5

Slam the trunk shut,
resume positions and quest,
only for a following sedan
to draw ever closer.
We must protect the dyad,
and protect the child,

but we cannot outrun this,
we must face them.
Confrontation ensues,
we hide the child,
we speak our truth,
advocate for the dyad;
and obtain release.

6

Another traveller senses it,
danger again, but danger within,
something is treacherous,
this must be excised.
Three of us challenge
the apparition,
its silver knife flashes,
I wrench the blade free,
it reaches for the seams of its shroud,
but the others are too fast,
razor sharp quills are seized.
I stab over and over;
it vanishes and we are now nine.

7

Realization dawns,
sickening and sudden:
for many miles we've
been going the wrong way.
Who read the map?
Our vanquished wraith?
No one knows.
Despair sidles up.
But look—see here,
a port within reach:
carry on, seek to
take ship from there.

8

The tang of sea air fills the senses,
but stay alert, threat still stalks
and we need money for passage.
Just one opportunity asks no questions:
design communiqués,
crank them out on
an archaic printing press.
Remembered youth flowing,
I take control, lay out a page,
then joined by an elder
from a dimension unseen
with another sheet, and
we race to finish.

9

We two fall to chatting,
realize the dyad's story must be told,
the nightmare laid bare.
There is one priceless picture,
just one, simple,
but it can hint,
it might warn:
a glowering wall,
petrified sandbags
scarred with inlaid
gaping skulls and
surmounted by razor wire;
we will duplicate it,
insinuate into the narrative;
the truth will be honoured,
the silence ended;
the unseen dimension calls the elder back
and I am left alone with the travellers
and the creation.

10

Passage has been earned,
the ship about to sail,
emanation is at hand;
we nine are all there,
dyad and child and sextet,
we kaleidoscope review and expectation.
An exhausted and relieved
sun rises behind me,
memory sparks dance on waiting waves.

Contemplations

Boats Against the Current

with F. Scott Fitzgerald

...borne back ceaselessly into the past
(a lure and a trap, a prison and a refuge),
seduced by eddies of nostalgia, pride and regret,
engulfed by whirlpools of obsession, bygone joy, and trauma,
we quest for the lost or never gained,
so we beat on, boats against the current,
resist time's onward rush as
we hunt for the ephemeral key.

And one fine morning—drifting awake,
the moment seems right, it's just there,
but floats out of reach again
so *tomorrow we will run faster,*
stretch out our arms farther...
and grasp not an answer but a phantom,
not what we once so deeply desired but a mirage.

It eluded us then, but that's no matter—
for what was it but a fantasy of *the*
orgiastic future that year by year recedes before us.
Driven, or maybe surrendering, into a new old course
we inevitably are turned forward
leaving the beguiling shadows behind.

Gatsby believed in the green light,
his green light, an unattainable dream
beckoning across the water, as each of us
is consumed with finding our own beacon,
afraid it's lost in the shades of
unreachable yesterdays, hoping it may yet
be over the horizon that pulls us irresistibly
on under the night.

On Contemplating a Ruined Abbey

Cragged bones thrust out of English countryside,
naked stony roots reaching
for absolution and completion
amidst meadow and rain,
under sun and avian serenade.
Fascinated from the first,
I wander through,
and in peaceful moments
lost, archaic memories are still here,
flitting and whispering in the shadows:
resting places for venerable relics,
quiet cloisters and cells,
chant-echoing sculpted walls and ceilings,
all raised by faith
for beautification
and celebration
and glorification;
a monument to humility and simplicity
endowed with wealth and privilege:
For here too were money and treasures
petrifying lifetimes of humble labour,
and power conferred by
possession and churchly authority;
a glittering and prideful tide
that drove humble spirit to lonely corners;
until swept in a jealous king and his minions
hungering for riches to support worldly affairs,
grasping for ecclesiastical domination,
no resistance brooked,
the shrine to divine glory
rendered a desecrated shell
for the greed of later times
to pillage even further.

Those naked cragged bones endure,
stripped of edificial flesh and sinew,
open air embraced,
granting space for reveried reconstruction,
beckoning to be clothed in vision.
Once superior and sealed off,
now exposed and accessible,
once witness to violence and avarice,
now intimating peaceful vulnerability,
stony supplicants forever in communion
with all of Creation.

A Tunnel at Vimy

Mid-30's Canadian monument perched at
ridge-top towers over Douai plain below,
twin pinnacles piercing sky,
huge pedestal graced with
names of thousands who
    vanished into war's maw
and statues of various meaning,
the foremost, her head drooped in mourning,
blind to the view for which so many perished.

A kilometre behind her, much newer,
the Visitor's Centre, helpful young staff
from home, and contextual displays,
nestled amongst clusters of craters,
smaller from artillery,
bigger from miners deep underground
planting explosives rather than
extracting copper and coal,
the grass here cropped by light-footed sheep
who glide over any hibernating munitions.
And, just behind, restored trenches,
    sandbags now concrete;
the two sides here shockingly close,
near enough to wave hello
(or goodbye).

Here also is the tunnel tour's start,
through a locked door and
down, ingested by a reclaimed,
tiny portion of the original labyrinth,
tourist-smooth underfoot, far better lit now,
(unrestored, ungentrified side passage
hints at original rugged darkness)
but chalky walls still exude dank and cool;
the miner's domain many metres lower still.
Today—only us twelve slipping by ghosts;

in April 1917—many, many more, jammed in,
waiting for their throw of the dice
against the unconquered heights,
awash with memories of months of preparation,
from night raids to a replica battlefield;
waiting along seven kilometres of front,
awash with memories of homes
from Victoria to Truro,
        Montreal to Winnipeg,
        London to Regina,
this tunnel echoing then with stories of
Toronto, Edmonton and beyond;
waiting hour after hour after hour
amidst artillery's unending crumps
reverberating through the chalk;
waiting, and leaving a mark,
inscribed names (HAYLER all caps and bold)
and symbols (over there a simple maple leaf),
all with one message: I was here, I mattered;
waiting to explode into a broken world of
mud and blood, barbed wire and
bullets impaling the snow and sleet
while this day's foe were shrouded in
their own tunnels and trenches under a
hail of shells dubbed the Week of Suffering;
all awaiting fate's verdict, some to
become a name on a monument wall,
    or on a headstone,
or remembered by one saying only
    Known Unto God,
others to survive this day
(perhaps wounded in body or soul),
those in our tunnel to be
hailed as victors.

Back in the gray light we wander
maimed terrain, now with a coverlet of Nature
    to soften lurking agony,
finding the well-kept cemetery quiet, no other visitors,
only bees peacefully circulating amongst
fresh clover between the graves,
gathering precious nectar and spreading new life.

Inconclusion

with Emily Dickinson

This World is not Conclusion.
Though, some seem to wish it were;
a declaration that
> *A Species stands beyond—*
> *Invisible, as Music—*
> *But positive, as Sound—*
violates theory and belief, so such
dissenters are bestowed an
epistolary bash or a pitying glance
while the troupe marches on,
revealing much, expanding scholarship,
but not truly hearing.
An enlightening quest, yet
on the way old lessons are forgotten:
> If God-seeking Aquinas proved anything
> it was that Reason, mighty and indispensable,
> still remains a tool, not an end;
and newer ones not appreciated:
> Gödel's analytical earthquake is inescapable,
> all logical castles, no matter how marvellous,
> eventually crack on an unprovable block
> or subterranean contradiction.

Thus the brilliant, blinkered journey continues,
but that ghostly Music remains,
> *It beckons, and it baffles—*
so they strain every filament,
pluck at any *twig of evidence* that
might reduce a wonder to a by-product,
spin up epicycles on atoms to explain all;
the borehole is sunk ever deeper,
uncovering and illuminating even more, only
to find a quantum haze at the foundations
and a singular mystery at the start; truly
> *through a Riddle, at the last—*
> *Sagacity, must go—*

Amidst this rush of progress and knowledge,
    elemental and cosmic,
it may ultimately be found that,
in the depths of quiet,
        Narcotics cannot still the Tooth
        That nibbles at the soul—

slender fire races

under my skin[1]

To Sappho

someone will remember us
I say
even in another time[2]

---

[1] *From Sappho, Fragment 31, translated by Willis Barnstone 2009*

[2] *Sappho, Fragment 147, translated by Anne Carson 2002*

Sappho, Ethereal Muse

Tantalizing bits float to us on Time's breezes,
survivors of Caesar's fireships at Alexandria,
      Papal book burning,
      various sackings,
      Theban need for coffin linings,
      and old-fashioned neglect,
but these ragged scraps of papyrus,
      morsels quoted by others,
      and an engraved potsherd
glow and tease with lyrical genius
birthed in an ancient land of
    vineyards, olive groves, orchards and crags.

Revered of old as the Tenth Muse,
no martial masculine voice this, rather
feminine, personal, tender and reflective;
and unashamedly desirous of other women:
      scandal for later narrow minds,
      inspiration for distant sisters.

A gift to eternity,
her splinters of light still illumine
    both Nature and the intimate,
these scattered sparkling stars
an elegy for, and a promise of,
a glorious ethereal firmament.

For Aphrodite, Wherever She May Be

Where are you now?
Sappho knew, all those centuries ago; invited you
from Kriti to her temple graced with apple trees,
altars fragrant with frankincense and
horses grazing in a flower-garlanded meadow.
My inducements are much more modest.
No perfumed shrine, and the lovely great pastures
are now mostly paved over.

I do hold onto a small plot, not what you are used to,
not for a long while redolent of youth,
but maybe there are other beauties,
enticing in their own way.
There's even a tiny meadow; I'm proud of that.
No lovely horses, but lots of squirrels,
the occasional rabbit or raccoon, or even a groundhog;
and plenty of my bird friends.
As for your love of apple trees, I do understand.
Long ago I claimed an old orchard as my own;
slipped away alone, child though I was,
to wander its quiet rows,
swing on welcoming branches,
caress the gnarled trunks.
Sadly, another sacrifice to modernity,
they've been gone many years, except
in my heart, where they blossom anew.
Alas then, no apple trees here, but
two magnificent oaks shelter my little woodland
and a natal patch of luscious blackberries.

So, wherever you may be,
wherever you have taken refuge,
a humble grove awaits;
come leaven this offering
with your special joy.

So

So a lost, lonely one
longs to be you

Bereft

The three a.m. train's
echoing wails fade over the
frozen yards leaving me
alone once more.

Genesis

Come long-absent showers
a desert blooms—
glowing embers of colour
illuminating her, one
familiar as yesterday but
seen through new eyes,
as near and as untouchable
as tomorrow, all this
Aphrodite's private gift
and torment.

Slender Fire

She is near—
for me, nearer than breath,
yet far beyond reach,
no closer than the stars,
since, alas, no goddess attributes
have I, save portrayal of calm.
Then comes
        a soft word,
            an unknowingly sensuous gesture,
        a precious touch,
and the ancient slender fire
is reborn and races under my skin,
scalding all senses,
inflaming mind and heart;
but I am bound by cold chains
invisible, and unbreakable,
and soon am left with
only flickering cinders,
a wistful memorial to
desire and suffering,
expectant, but in despair.

Before Dawn

Before Lady Dawn enwraps
the gloaming with golden arms,
and before the robin chimes the morning song,
visions sweep in on phantasmic wings,
oft dark and dreary, fearsome and formidable,
but some few apparelled in tender, sultry light,
Eros calling in the depths of slumber's spell,
offering up an ethereal taste of climactic nectar.

Erasure

Deep in sleep's domain,
following Eros' summons,
the only route to   ;
for she is there,   ,
        mirror, but beautiful,
in an elysian realm
            outsiders   swept away,
            the past fades, the future steps back;
            looks   linger,
                                        smoulder,
                            catch fire;
where a fleeting touch pauses,
        shrinks   ,
        then returns   ,
                            to a caress
                wonder and exhilaration;
lips   ,
searching,   while
        dance and play,
clothes   ,
            and
graze and knead,

        wind, flow and merge
finally blazing forth   ecstatic   ,
found only here, deep in sleep's domain,
enmeshed in Eros' chimerical webs.

Confronting Old Age

Quicksilver youth nimbly skip from
the tangible to the conceptual,
easily grasp both thought and pickle jar.
The years have laid siege to my
joints and organs,
encumbered mind and hands,
skipping and grasping now
slower and pain-attended.
I attempt a cloak of wisdom and
deploy meds and complaints,
but what, really, can be done?
The way of aging is laid before us.
Tolkien says that even Arwen Undómiel,
dazzling for millennia,
once she opted for humanity was
yoked to the mortal path.

Cicada

Song's desire is universal
but expression is
a variegated gift—
varied too are the cues.
At summer's apotheosis
heat and light insist that
autumn can wait.
Nature bursts with possibility,
aching for serenade, and
into the breach steps the cicada.
Unlovely to many, beloved by a few,
its insistent voice a shrill buzz
to some ears, yet listen deeper,
the language unfamiliar, the means exotic,
but a chorus of heartfelt alleluias nonetheless.

Welcome—sing the celebration for us.

Evening Star

Sappho's Hesperos, twilight's flaming diamond,
guardian of the portals of night—
lifting my eyes, I am inescapably beckoned,
following so many through the eons:
the weary labourer awash in long-sought relief
under the spell of sleep's harbinger;
a child gazing up in wonder at the
herald of emerging heavenly glories;
the overdue traveller guided onward
by firmament's wanderer.
And my wish ineluctably drawn—
may you shepherd us roaming spirits
homeward to peace and rest at last.

Acknowledgements

My sincere thanks to Richard Grove (Tai) and Wet Ink Books, Muriel Allingham, Andreas Gripp, Penn Kemp, John B. Lee, Felicia Otchet, David Stones, Jane Twynham and Murray Winger, and my family.

My thanks also to the following where versions of the listed poems first appeared:

Beliveau Review: Nocturne

Ekphrastic Review: Pollock's Dance

It's Your Move, by David, June and Marcie Wenn: This Moment

Journey of the Heart: Evening Star

Poems in Response to Peril Anthology: Kaleidoscope for the Invasion of Ukraine, February 24 2022

Shot Glass Journal: Genesis

Stones Beneath the Surface Anthology: Triplicity

Stratford Quarterly: Hannah's Lament

Synaeresis: Crickets, A Tunnel at Vimy

WordCity Literary Journal: The Ballad of Margaret Murphy, Crossing Lines, One Malignant Spirit

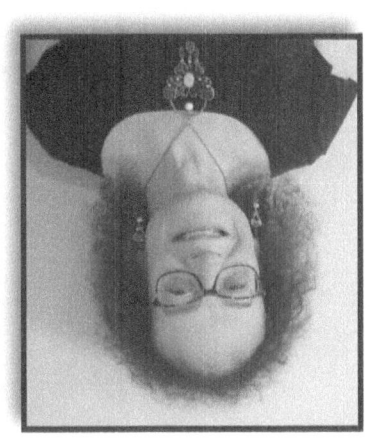

Biographical Note:

Jennifer Wenn is a trans-identified writer and speaker from London, Ontario, who was selected honorary Grand Marshall for London's 2023 Pride Parade. Her first poetry chapbook, *A Song of Milestones*, was published by Harmonia Press. Her first full-size collection, *Hear Through the Silence*, was published by Cyberwit. She has also written *From Adversity to Accomplishment* (a family and social history) and published poetry in numerous journals and anthologies, including *WordCity Literary Journal*, *The Ekphrastic Review*, *Synaeresis*, *Journey of the Heart*, *Open Minds Quarterly*, *Shot Glass Journal* and *Qutub Minar Review*, and the anthologies *Poems in Response to Peril*, *Dénouement*, *Stones Beneath the Surface* and *Things That Matter*. She has published reviews and articles in *Scarlet Leaf Review*, *The Miramichi Reader*, *Tuck Magazine*, the *League of Canadian Poets National Poetry Month* (Jennifer is a full member) and *centred.ca*. She is also on the Board of Antler River Poetry and the proud parent of two adult children.

Visit her website at:
https://jenniferwennpoet.wixsite.com/home